LAWS
AGAINST
SEXUAL AND
DOMESTIC VIOLENCE

*A Concise Guide
for Clergy and Laity*

Mary S. Winters, J.D.

Lonni Collins Pratt
518 W. Nepessing Suite 201
Lapeer, MI 48446

THE PILGRIM PRESS
NEW YORK

Copyright © 1988 The Pilgrim Press
All rights reserved
No part of this publication may be reproduced, stored in a retrieval system, or transmitted in any form or by any means, electronic, mechanical, photocopying, recording, or otherwise (brief quotations used in magazine or newspaper reviews excepted), without the prior permission of the publisher.

The biblical quotations in this book are from the *Revised Standard Version of the Bible*, copyright 1946, 1952, and © 1971, 1973 by the Division of Christian Education, National Council of Churches, and are used by permission.

Library of Congress Cataloging-in-Publication Data

Winters, Mary S., 1950–
    Laws against sexual and domestic violence.
    Bibliography: p. 49.
    1. Family violence—Law and legislation—United States—Popular works. 2. Sex crimes—United States—Popular works. 3. Child abuse—Law and legislation—United States—Popular works. 4. Family violence—United States. 5. Child molesting—United States. 6. Church work with families—United States. I. Title.
KF9320.W56 1988   344.73′03282   88-9930
ISBN 0-8298-0780-2 (pbk.)   347.3043282

The Pilgrim Press, 132 West 31 Street, New York, NY 10001

Contents

Foreword by Faith A. Johnson   v

I. Introduction

A. Facts and Statistics on Sexual and Domestic Violence   1
B. Definitions of Sexual and Domestic Violence   4
C. Cultural Judgments and Myths Versus the Realities of Domestic Violence   5
D. The United Church of Christ's Pronouncement on Violence Against Women   7
E. Sexual and Domestic Violence and the Legal System as Remedy   9

II. Domestic and Sexual Violence Against Adults

A. Domestic Violence   12
    1. *Options for the Victim of Domestic Violence* 12
    2. *What to Do Before, During, and After the Attack* 16
    3. *Battered Women and Self-defense* 19
    4. *Options for the Batterer or Defendant in a Domestic Violence Situation* 20
    5. *Questions and Answers on Domestic Violence, the Law, and You, the Victim of Domestic Violence* 20
       Finding an Attorney 22
       Finding a Mediator 23
    6. *Description of Steps and Other Definitions in the Law on Domestic Violence* 24
    7. *Abuse of Older People and the Disabled* 25
B. Sexual Violence Against Adults: Rape   27
    1. *Introduction* 27
    2. *Options for the Rape Victim* 28
    3. *Options for the Accused Rapist* 29
    4. *Questions and Answers on Sexual Assault, the Law, and You, the Victim of Sexual Assault* 29
C. Sexual Harassment in the Workplace   31

III. Domestic and Sexual Violence Against Children
A. Child Abuse   32
    1. *Introduction*   32
    2. *Definitions of Child Abuse*   32
    3. *Typical State Statute Prohibiting Child Abuse*   32
    4. *Options in a Child Abuse Situation*   33
    5. *The Case Against Spanking Children*   35
B. Sexual Abuse of Children   36
    1. *Definitions*   36
    2. *What You Can Do*   36

IV. How Church Members and Ministers Can Work Against Violence in Our Society
A. Work Against Bias Against Women in the Court System   39
B. Develop Helping Relationships with Both the Abused and the Abuser   40
C. What New York State Has Done: Suggestions for Lobbying Initiatives   40
D. Advocate Within the Church Against Sexual and Domestic Violence   42
E. Work Within the Church Against Child Abuse and Sexual Assault   43
F. Recommendations for Preventing and Remedying Abuse of Older People   44
G. Advocate Against Sexual and Domestic Violence in the Larger Society   45

V. Resources
A. Hot Lines   47
B. Organizations   47
C. Publications   49

Appendix: The United Church of Christ's Pronouncement on Violence Against Women   51

Foreword

Church-related people would like to believe that sexual and domestic violence occurs in the lives of other people, that the Christian message of justice and love insulates people from such offenses. In fact, some clergy who have served parishes for many years truly believe that sexual and domestic violence has not occurred in any of the parishes they have served. However, several pastors who have held such convictions have been shocked to find that mention of such violence in a sermon enables parishioners to confess that they were being violated or that they were violating their spouses and/or children. Until the pastor broke the silence, parishioners felt compelled to keep the secret.

This guide offers assistance to clergy who want to be helpful to parish members who have suffered violation or perpetrated violence and who want to know how the law relates to her or his situation. The guide also challenges the church members to advocate for legal and social services that can give effective assistance to both victims and offenders.

According to the surgeon general, battering is the major cause of injury among women in the United States. Battered women, and children as well, sit in our pews on Sunday; they are our neighbors; they are our friends. This guide will assist church-related people in understanding the laws that protect them, to advocate for better laws. I hope that it will stimulate clergy and concerned laity to supplement this guide with guides to their own state and local laws relating to such crimes.

—Faith A. Johnson
Secretary for Human Development
Division of the American Missionary Association
United Church Board for Homeland Ministries

For Her

It should be noted that this book is intended as a guide and does not constitute legal advice.

» I «
Introduction

A. *Facts and Statistics on Sexual and Domestic Violence*

Sexual and domestic violence is only too common, whether it is spouse or partner abuse, rape, child abuse, sexual abuse of children—including incest—or abuse of older people. Such violence occurs at an appalling rate between people of every religion, race and ethnicity, age, socioeconomic situation, and educational level; among all life-styles; and in every region and part of the United States, whether urban, suburban, or rural. There is no evading the fact, however, that sexual and domestic violence in our homes and in the larger society is most frequently directed against women and children—particularly girls—by men. This fact is reflected in the preponderant use of the masculine pronoun for the abuser and the feminine pronoun for the victim of sexual and domestic violence in this guide. Sexual and domestic violence is wrong. It is an abuse of power that destroys the soul and psyche of both the abused and the abuser; it can cause physical and psychological injuries that result in permanent impairment and death; and it destroys relationships and families. To worsen the tragedy of sexual and domestic violence, recent research has shown that young victims of such violence often grow up to become abusers themselves.

Consider the following facts and statistics on the frequency of sexual and domestic violence, crimes for which our society tends to blame the victim.

DOMESTIC VIOLENCE

1. A report by the National League of Cities and the U.S. Conference of Mayors notes: "The incidence of wife assault is so pervasive in this society that half of all wives will experience some form of spouse-inflicted violence during their marriage, regardless of race or socio-economic status."
2. The FBI estimates that a woman is beaten by a man every 18 seconds in this country. The number of wife beatings reported is three times more

prevalent than reported rapes. Wife-beating is considered the single most under-reported crime in the country.
  3. One-third to one-fourth of the homicides in the United States are between a spouse killing a spouse.
  4. Police receive more calls for help from victims of domestic violence than from victims of any other serious crime.*
  5. Battered husbands or male partners appear to be a fraction of 1% of battered spouses or partners.†

CHILD ABUSE

  1. Almost 2 million American children are victims of child abuse each year.
  2. In one year alone, 1 million parents used a knife or gun to threaten or injure their child, and an estimated 2,000 to 5,000 children die each year as a direct result of child abuse.
  3. Murder is the primary cause of death for children under five years. One child is killed each day in the United States by a family member.
  4. A survey of over 2,000 families found that the rate of child abuse is 129% higher in families where there is also spousal abuse. (Steinmetz, Straus and Gelles, 1975).‡

SEXUAL ABUSE OF CHILDREN

  1. One in four females under 18 years will be sexually abused by someone well known to the child.
  2. The American Humane Association found that girls constituted 87% of the child victims of sexual abuse. Seventy-five percent of the offenders were household members, relatives, friends, or neighbors known to the child.
  3. A recent study by the State of Arizona found that in approximately 90% of reported sexual assaults on children, child pornography was found in the attacker's residence.§

PARENT ABUSE AND ABUSE OF OLDER PEOPLE

  1. Children in one out of 10 American families hit, beat, stab, or shoot their parents.

---

* "Dealing with Domestic Violence," Community Mediation Program of OUR TOWN Family Center, Tucson, Arizona, 1986. Used by permission.
† Ministry to Abusive Families, Family Resource Series, Division for Parish Services, Lutheran Church in America.
‡ "Dealing with Domestic Violence."
§ Ibid.

2. Out of 28 million Americans over 60 years of age, more than one million older parents will be abused by their own children this year.

3. Research by Richard Gelles indicates that there are 4.7 million families in the United States in which at least one parent is the victim of physical violence by a child.

4. Gelles' data show that most of the children—largely teenagers—who beat their parents were themselves beaten as children.*

Many people unfamiliar with the dynamics of sexual and domestic violence wonder why women and others do not simply leave abusive relationships. Battered women can get trapped with a violent spouse or partner owing to a complex mix of powerful emotions and compelling social and economic pressures. For example, an abused woman who stays in an abusive relationship can experience strong physical and psychological fear of her partner and, at the same time, little or no protection from the police or court system. She also is ashamed of and humiliated by her "failure" as a wife and mother, even when with friends, family members, and physician. She probably has a low self-esteem, and may be overly passive and emotionally dependent. Women who stay with abusive partners probably grew up with the damaging and erroneous belief that women are weak and inferior to men and should therefore submit to them in return for financial support for themselves and their children. Plus, an abused woman often continues to hope that the abuser will abandon his abusive behavior, which seldom, if ever, happens without professional help.

Along with her own emotions, a battered woman can be trapped by external factors. Many abused women—as well as abusers—experience severe isolation; some battered women may not realize that they are victims of a terrible wrong. Others may experience family pressures: they believe that their children need a father or male in the home no matter how defective a role model he is, or their own families may disapprove of divorce or separation under any circumstances. The statistically typical battered woman married young and has several young children. If she leaves her abusive partner, she and her children face impoverishment. If she does not leave but has her husband or partner arrested, he may lose his job. Furthermore, a battered woman may also be discouraged by her perception of societal attitudes that blame the victim of sexual and domestic violence, or by authority figures who urge the battered

* Ibid.

woman to "forgive and forget" to keep the family together. For these very real reasons, most battered women suffer repeated attacks, usually for years, before they try to escape from an abusive relationship.

Children stay in abusive homes because they are the only environment the children know; because they are afraid to tell anyone about the abuse; because they are economically dependent on their parents; because they love and need their parents—the abusive behavior may be only part of their relationship; and because they may believe the myths about battering or incest that our society believes: that the victims are to blame and are "bad people." They feel alone and without help.

B. *Definitions of Sexual and Domestic Violence*

Workers in this field have asserted that domestic violence against adults—including the aged—and children can be expressed in at least five ways: physical violence, sexual violence, psychological violence, economic abuse, and as violence toward objects or pets that belong to the abused person.

» *Physical violence* involves the use of weapons, such as guns and knives, and/or the abuser's body, such as hitting, spanking, choking, shoving, biting, slapping, and kicking.

» *Sexual violence* is related to physical violence, but it has specifically sexual characteristics. Adult-child incest and rape, including rape by a stranger or an acquaintance, and marital rape, belong in this category. The majority of women who report physical abuse also report incidents of sexual abuse. Similarly, there is a high correlation between the sexual abuse of children and the physical abuse of their mothers.

» *Psychological abuse* is less readily defined, although many abusive behavior patterns fall into this category. Verbal abuse, coercion, and threats; intimidation; public humiliation; being locked out of the house; having money or car keys taken; being refused help in cases of sickness, injury, or pregnancy; or any act or words that create a climate of fear and psychic pressure constitute psychological abuse. An accompanying behavior is often enforced isolation. The victim's freedom is restricted such that her or his ability to contact those who could give support is reduced.

>> *Economic abuse* includes behaviors such as hoarding and the withholding of family financial information from the abused.

>> *Destruction of the abused's pets or property* by the abuser represents both an implied threat to the victim and a devaluing of what the victim values.

An important clarification: All these experiences, whether physical, sexual, psychological, economically abusive, or destructive of property, are experiences not of conflict, but of violence. Conflict is disagreement and tension, but it is not the same as violence. Conflict does not necessarily escalate into violence.* For example, stress has been a recurrent finding for both the abused and the abuser in cases of abuse of older people. But although stress seems to be an "intensifier" for potential abuse, it is not a clear predictor for abuse, since most families that undergo stress do not abuse their older members.† It is not true that any person can be driven to violence if faced with a sufficiently stressful and provoking situation. All of us experience conflict and pain in our relationships at times, which, if effectively dealt with, can lead to growth and greater harmony in the relationship. Abusive people, however, wrongfully use violence in situations in which others would choose not to, and with no positive outcome possible.

Another important clarification made by victims' advocates is that there is no "scale" of violence. Violence cannot be accurately defined as "mild" or "severe." One blow establishes a climate of fear between the batterer and the abused in which the threat of further violence is perpetually real and present. Furthermore, a "gentle" shove down the stairs can be fatal. Any violence or fear of violence in an intimate relationship is out of place.‡

C. *Cultural Judgments and Myths Versus the Realities of Domestic Violence*

Myths about domestic violence tend to blame the person being beaten instead of the person doing the beating. As a result, women who are abused

---

* Based on "Final Report, Dialogue on the Mediation of Violent Family and Relational Conflicts," October 12–14, 1986, sponsored by the Interfaith Conciliation Center, Mt. Vernon, New York.

† Margaret F. Hudson and Tanya F. Johnson, "A Critical Review of Research on Elder Neglect and Abuse," *The Annual Review of Gerontology and Geriatrics* 6, 1986.

‡ See "Final Report, Dialogue on the Mediation of Violent Family and Relational Conflicts."

in our society often end up believing that it is their fault and that they could control the violence if they only tried harder.

CULTURAL JUDGMENTS AND MYTHS

Battered women deserve to be beaten because of the way they behave. They "ask for it."

REALITIES

No one deserves to be beaten no matter what one does. The dynamics of violence in the family are complex. However, men who abuse do so because of their own internal reasons, not because of the actions of their partners. Men who abuse find it difficult to take responsibility for their own behavior.

Women who are abused like it. Otherwise they wouldn't stay.

No one likes being slapped, shoved, choked, hit, or kicked. But it is difficult for a woman to leave if she has no place to go and no money or means of support, or if the man has sworn to kill her if she ever leaves.

Drinking causes violent behavior.

There is no doubt that some association exists between drinking and violent behavior. Many women believe that if the drinking stopped, the battering would cease. However, alcohol is just part of the reason a partner is abusive. Abusers are potentially violent not only when they are under the influence of alcohol, but also when they are sober.

Only poor and uneducated families experience violence, and minority women are battered more frequently than Anglo women.

Battering is a crime that cuts across all ethnic and socioeconomic groups. Since middle- and upper-class women often have other options open to them, they are less likely to seek help from public agencies and thus to appear in public statistics. Anglo and minority women alike experience abuse. However, minority women report having fewer resources to turn to for assistance.

Domestic violence affects only a small percentage of the overall population.

While the extent of abuse is unknown, one comprehensive nationwide study found that 28% of the couples interviewed reported violence at some point in their relationship.

Men who are abusive are violent in most of their relationships, are generally unsuccessful, and lack abilities to cope with the world. They are often described as "losers."

> Approximately 80% of the men who batter their partners are not violent in other aspects of their lives. In one study of 120 battered women, the batterers were indistinguishable from any other group of men in terms of capability.

Boys from violent homes grow up to be batterers, girls to be victims.

> While it is true that childhood experiences with violence tend to increase the likelihood of becoming involved in abusive relationships as adults, abusers and victims also come from nonviolent homes. In addition, not everyone who is raised in a violent environment will become abusive or victimized as an adult.

Once a batterer, always a batterer.

> There are counseling programs for the batterer, which assist him in finding nonviolent solutions to problems. However, it is important to realize that studies indicate that the majority of batterers do not believe they need to change and so never seek counseling.

Domestic violence is a private, family affair. What goes on in one's own home is no one else's business.

> Assault is a criminal offense—regardless of the relationship between the parties involved. Violence within the family is as unjustifiable as violence in the streets.*

D. *The United Church of Christ's Pronouncement on Violence Against Women*

In 1983 the United Church of Christ brought forth a Pronouncement on Violence Against Women at its 14th General Synod. The Pronouncement represents the most straightforward and af-

---

* Compiled for the Southern Arizona Task Force on Domestic Violence by Irene Anderson, Linda Hale Barter, and Ann Yellott, August 1986. References used: Massachusetts Coalition of Battered Women Service Groups *For Shelter and Beyond*, 1981. Lenore E. Walker, *The Battered Woman*, 1979; Myrna M. Zambrano, *Mejor Sola Que Mal Acompañada: Para La Mujer Golpeada*, 1985. Reprinted, with permission, from "Dealing with Domestic Violence," Community Mediation Program of OUR TOWN Family Center, Tucson, Arizona, 1986.

firmative statement produced by any Protestant denomination in the U.S. in an effort to speak to this common experience of women. In this regard, the UCC gives evidence of its willingness to hear the truth of our experience of personal violence as women and to fulfill its responsibility to speak to it theologically, ethically, and pastorally.

The Pronouncement sets forth the UCC's commitment to a comprehensive response which will include three necessary dimensions: the pastoral, the prophetic, and the preventive. The pastoral response encompasses the needs of victims of violence for a sensitive and informed pastoral support from both clergy and lay persons. The prophetic describes the need for a vocal and unambiguous truthtelling to break the silence which surrounds violence against women. The truth must be told about sexual abuse in the family, about violence against women of color, about violence in lesbian relationships, about violence against elderly women, about abuse and exploitation of women parishioners by their pastors—these particular forms of violence, long shrouded in silence and disbelief, must be spoken about openly. The preventive response is the activity which addresses the root sources of violence against women in ways which can prevent its recurrence. These root sources include sex role socialization, advertising and entertainment media, child and adult pornography, resistance to sexuality education, racism, classism, sexism, and militarism.

This Pronouncement provides the UCC with a tool to mobilize its resources to bring an end to all forms of violence against women. In doing so, the UCC joins with other people of faith in creating a new moral norm which will not tolerate the injustice of violence against women any longer, which names the sin for what it is, which seeks protection and healing for its victims, accountability for its perpetrators, and reconciliation in the community.

SUMMARY

As Christians, believing in the sacredness of God's creation and in the equality of women and men, we are called to speak out against the physical and/or sexual abuse of any person. Because women are the primary victims of domestic violence, rape, and sexual harassment, this Pronouncement calls for the United Church of Christ to increase its understanding of violence against women, provide ministry to victims and abusers, and work against violence in our society.*

---

*See Appendix for complete text of pronouncement.

E. Sexual and Domestic Violence and the Legal System as Remedy

Significant differences exist as to what constitutes the most appropriate method to remedy domestic violence. Possibilities include mediation between abuser and abused facilitated by an independent third party; advocacy by a third person who helps the victim to obtain relief from various sources by offering support and information; and/or the victim's recourse to the criminal justice system.

Advocates for women and children have asserted that mediation may present a trap in which power inequities and lack of protection can only further the violence and pain experienced by victims. In mediation, victims' advocates assert, the crimes of sexual and domestic violence are wrongfully made only an issue of private, rather than public, concern, in which the abuser is protected by confidentiality.

The criminal justice system has been criticized by victims of sexual and domestic violence on the following grounds:

» It is too limited to punitive actions carried out in an adversarial setting.
» It too strictly defines, and thus limits, issues addressed to those covered by actual charges against the abuser.
» It focuses unproductively on the past, merely to ascribe blame.
» It is rendered less effective by institutionalized attitudes of sexism, racism, and class-consciousness.

Nevertheless, at the Interfaith Conciliation Center dialogue event on the appropriate use of mediation in domestic violence situations held October 12-14, 1986 in Covington, Kentucky, participants agreed that the criminal justice system remains a necessary resource for victims of sexual and domestic violence, despite its need for improvement.

In response to society's growing awareness of the evil of domestic violence, many states and localities have specially trained police units that effectively help to handle cases of spouse or partner abuse. Several states have modified their laws to make it easier to arrest batterers. At least one study has found that arresting an offender was far more effective in preventing future assaults than two other common police approaches: ordering the offender to leave the house for eight hours and offering counseling.* But only a small percentage of those arrested are ever prosecuted because the charges are reduced to minor infractions of the law, or suspended sentences are recommended to the court by prosecutors, and judges in domestic violence cases often impose either a light sentence or no sentence. Nor can court orders of protection always safeguard battered women, since police do not provide a twenty-four-hour-a-day guard to women who have been granted a protection order. In a 1987 New York case, Karen Straw was tried—and acquitted—for stabbing to death her estranged husband, from whom she had suffered years of physical and psychological abuse, culminating in his rape of her at knifepoint in front of the two children. Ms. Straw had availed herself of all the legal options open to her: she had moved out of their home; filed formal complaints with the police; pressed charges for assault; and obtained several orders of protection. Ironically, Ms. Straw was impliedly criticized by the prosecution for not getting a legal separation or divorce from her abusive husband, which wrongfully suggested to the jury that she was at fault or that the abuse was not really all that serious because Mr. Straw was her husband. (Ms. Straw did indeed want a divorce but could not afford to seek one.)

Nevertheless, "while sexist attitudes and other serious problems still prevail in many cases, if a woman does decide to go to court, she will find there is more public and judicial support than ever for prosecuting violence against women."† There is also a greater likelihood of finding doctors, lawyers, judges, police, and counselors who can deal sensitively and effectively with the problem of domestic violence. Legislative reform has further empowered women to report violence, press charges, and appear as witnesses.

Sexual as well as domestic violence constitutes criminal behavior. It is a crime for anyone to have forced sexual contact with another adult, or for any adult or teenager to have sexual contact with a child, either by force or with consent. Reporting sexual assaults helps both the victim and others. Sex offenders almost always repeat their crimes and seldom seek treatment voluntarily, so criminal prosecution is, in all probability, the most effective method of countering sexual assault.

* Study by the Minneapolis Police Department and the Police Foundation, 1981.
† NOW Legal Defense and Education Fund and Renée Cherow-O'Leary, *The State-by-State Guide to Women's Legal Rights* (New York: McGraw-Hill, 1987), p. 79.

Justice-making for victims of sexual and domestic violence involves our legal system, as well as social service agencies, religious institutions, and mental health services. This guide is primarily directed toward the most effective use of our legal system's methods for protecting the victim and ending sexual and domestic violence.

» II «
Domestic and Sexual Violence Against Adults

A. DOMESTIC VIOLENCE

1. *Options for the Victim of Domestic Violence**

Any victim of domestic violence should, at a minimum, call the police for immediate assistance and protection, and obtain any needed medical treatment, either in an emergency room or from a private physician. A battered woman's call to the police for assistance need not result in legal action. To call the police, do one of the following:

» Dial your area's three-digit emergency number, such as 911.
» Dial "0" (follows the number nine) for operator, to give the address at which help is needed.
» Call your local police precinct office. Check the white pages of your telephone directory under "police department," or call the directory assistance operator.

Under most state laws, there are three legal strategies for dealing with abuse:

» *Divorce or legal separation* from the abusive partner and obtaining any legal orders needed to protect the victim and her children.
» *Criminal prosecution* of the batterer. See the following question-and-answer section on criminal charges.
» *An order of protection* that requires the abuser to stop the abuse, threats, and harassment.
   • A juvenile or domestic relations court judge issues the order of protection after the abuser, either the victim's spouse or partner, has been served with a notice of the

---

* See NOW Legal Defense and Education Fund and Renée Cherow-O'Leary, *The State-by-State Guide to Women's Legal Rights* (New York: McGraw-Hill, 1987), pp. 78–83.

hearing, and a court hearing has been duly held. If you do not have a lawyer, the court clerk will help you complete the forms.
- A batterer will be in contempt of court if he violates the order, and can then be fined or jailed as a penalty. Call the police *immediately* if your attacker does not obey the terms of the order. Have your copy of the order ready to show the police.
- If children are involved, the protective order may also provide for custody, visitation, child support or payment of other expenses, and agreements between the spouses or partners with regard to living arrangements.
- In most states it is not necessary to file for divorce to qualify for an order of protection.

Other remedies for victims of domestic violence are as follows:

》 National toll-free hot line for battered women maintained by the National Coalition Against Domestic Violence: 1-800-333-7233.

》 Call your state's twenty-four-hour hot line for referrals to agencies that can assist victims of domestic violence. The numbers preceded by an 800 area code are toll-free.*

Alabama	(205) 767-3076	Louisiana	(504) 389-3001
Alaska	(907) 586-3650	Maine	(207) 623-3569
Arizona	(602) 258-5344	Maryland	(301) 268-4393
Arkansas	(501) 741-6167	Massachusetts	(617) 426-8492
California	(213) 392-9874	Michigan	(800) 292-3925
Colorado	(303) 394-2810	Minnesota	(612) 646-6177
Connecticut	(203) 524-5890	Mississippi	(601) 436-3809
Delaware	(302) 571-2660	Missouri	(314) 531-9101
Dist. of Columbia	(202) 529-5991	Montana	(406) 228-4435
Florida	(800) 342-9152	Nebraska	(402) 345-6555
Georgia	(912) 234-9999	Nevada	(702) 358-4214
Hawaii	(808) 538-7216	New Hampshire	(800) 852-3311
Idaho	(208) 334-2480	New Jersey	(800) 322-8092
Illinois	(800) 252-6561	New Mexico	(505) 526-2819
Indiana	(812) 334-8378	New York	(800) 942-6906
Iowa	(515) 288-1981	North Carolina	(919) 889-6636
Kansas	(800) 257-2255	North Dakota	(701) 255-6240
Kentucky	(606) 581-6282	Ohio	(614) 221-1255

* Provided by the National Coalition Against Domestic Violence, Washington, D.C.

Oklahoma	(800) 522-7233	Texas	(512) 482-8200
Oregon	(503) 239-4486	Utah	(801) 355-2846
Pennsylvania	(717) 652-9571	Vermont	(802) 748-8645
Puerto Rico	(809) 781-2570	Virginia	(804) 780-3505
Rhode Island	(401) 723-3051	Washington	(800) 562-6025
South Carolina	(803) 765-9428	West Virginia	(304) 645-6334
South Dakota	(605) 226-1212	Wisconsin	(608) 255-0539
Tennessee	(615) 623-3125	Wyoming	(307) 856-0942

Agencies or shelters that assist victims of domestic violence and their children can offer the following:
- A shelter or a safe home for you to stay in
- Twenty-four-hour hot line
- Counseling
- Advocacy with police, courts, and welfare system
- Children's counseling and other programs
- Job counseling and training
- Legal services
- Counseling for batterers
- Escort through government agencies
- Counselors who speak languages in addition to English
- Referrals to needed services, and assistance in finding an appropriate mediator, lawyer, or therapist
- Speakers' bureau and community outreach programs

>>> In a growing number of states, a battered woman may be able to seek money damages from the batterer in a civil lawsuit.
- This is monetary compensation that may cover medical bills, lost wages, loss of earning capacity, damage to property, pain and suffering, physical and psychological suffering, and permanent injuries, and that may also include purely punitive damages.
- A battered woman must usually prove physical and/or emotional damage through the use of evidence beyond her own statements. Such evidence might include objects or weapons used, color photographs of injuries taken as soon after the assault as possible, medical records, and a police report.
- Check with an attorney on the availability of this remedy in your state.

⟩⟩⟩ If the police or employees of criminal, civil, or family courts do not adequately assist a battered woman, a civil suit may be brought against these officials to compel them to perform their duty, or to obtain money damages for harm resulting to the victim of abuse from their failure to do so. Again, consult an attorney in your state.

⟩⟩⟩ Another remedy for battered women is available through awards of temporary alimony in divorce. Temporary alimony, sometimes called rehabilitative maintenance, is designed to enable a woman (or man) to gain, or regain, her economic independence through education, training, and therapy, and to avoid financial hardship during the rehabilitative process. Maintenance awarded for a limited period has been criticized as a means of forcing former full-time homemakers with no job skills into unemployment, underpaid jobs, or welfare.* Apart from the issue of the fairness and effectiveness of rehabilitative maintenance, a battered woman who is awarded this financial assistance should seek to have included in that amount funds for training in assertiveness skills, and for the restoration of her physical and mental health to a level that permits her to again function in the world without fear.

⟩⟩⟩ Another option for a battered woman is to stay in the abusive relationship. The abuse, however, is likely to become more frequent and severe *unless* outside help is sought to make basic improvements in the relationship.

- *Both* partners should get individual and couple counseling through a social service agency, women's center, batterers' group, court or legal aid society referral, or private therapist. Someone who is experienced with domestic violence may help the abusive spouse or partner control violent impulses, help the family deal with the psychic wounds of abuse, and help the woman protect herself and her children against violence.
- *Important:* Victims' advocates strongly urge that the following be noted where mediation is considered for problem-solving in an abusive relationship:

Mediation may indeed be an effective tool in settling family disputes and in equipping the family to deal with future disputes. However, when domestic violence occurs, protecting the victim and

---

* See Mary S. Winters, *Divorce Law: A Concise Guide for Clergy and Laity* (New York: The Pilgrim Press, 1986), pp. 13, 25–26.

stopping the abuse are the first steps. Mediation is not to be used as an initial intervention in a violent domestic situation. After the violence has ended, mediation may have the potential to bring healing and closure for both parties. Mediation should *never* be used at any time to mediate violence, as opposed to conflict. (Example of wrongful outcome of inappropriately mediated violence: "We agree that I will stop hitting you if you serve dinner on time.") Violence or psychological abuse in families or within relationships is never acceptable and is not negotiable.

>>> Mediators need to acknowledge and understand the power imbalance between men and women in favor of men, particularly the power imbalance created when violence exists in a relationship. Power imbalances can make mediation a wholly inappropriate option for dealing with any issue in a relationship, or with divorce or separation.*

>>> Mediation on any matter between a couple should not be court-mandated when there has been family violence.

>>> When abuse of children is uncovered or disclosed in mediation or any other context, protection of the child is the primary concern, and the abuse should be reported to the appropriate authorities. (See section on child abuse in this guide.)

>>> Victims' advocates note the sometimes inappropriate attraction that mediation has for religiously oriented people who see it as a compelling way to live out God's call that we be peacemakers and reconcilers. Without critical evaluation of mediation's strengths and weaknesses, the safety of victims may be compromised by a premature haste to seek reconciliation through mediation.†

2. *What to Do Before, During, and After the Attack*

>>> *Before the Attack:* Be prepared for you and your children to leave home quickly if you have experienced abuse or you fear abuse.
  • Pack a set of clothes for yourself and your children. Store the

---

* See Winters, *Divorce Law,* pp. 24–25.
† See "Final Report, Dialogue on the Mediation of Violent Family and Relational Conflicts," October 12–14, 1986, Sponsored by the Interfaith Conciliation Center, Mt. Vernon, NY.

- suitcase in the home of a friend or neighbor or hide it in your house where you can get to it easily.
- Have an extra set of car and house keys. Keep these hidden in your suitcase or another appropriate place.
- Collect and save evidence of your spouse's or partner's violent or abusive behavior. This evidence will be important in seeking legal remedies.
- Have in one accessible place any extra cash, savings, checkbooks, or other special valuables. This may help you to provide shelter and food for yourself and your children if you must leave your home.
- Take something familiar for the children, such as a toy or book.
- Take legal documents, such as identification, birth certificates, Social Security card, driver's license, marriage certificate, restraining order, documentation of car ownership.
- In summary, most important of all is to *plan ahead*. You can get advice and counseling from the battered women's shelter nearest you. Find out the telephone number of this shelter by calling your state's hot line number listed on pages 13-14.*

>>> *At the Time of Attack and Immediately After*
- Protect your face, chest, and abdomen, and do all you can to avoid intensifying the batterer's anger and hence violence.
- Leave as soon as you can and take the children. Not doing so may result in custody problems later.
- If you are unable to leave without assistance, call the police. See page 12.
- Document your injuries. Have them photographed when the injuries are most visible. This will be important in seeking legal remedies.
- Seek crisis services at a women's and children's shelter. Get a referral from the police or through the hot line numbers on pages 13-14.

>>> *Once the Crisis Is Over*
- Seriously reflect on your relationship with your abusive spouse or partner, and decide what to do. Then do it. Once you make a

---

* Based on the State of New Jersey, Department of Community Affairs and the Division on Women, *Domestic Violence: The Law and You* (Trenton, NJ: 1982), p. 6.

decision, there are many resources to help you build a new life. Ask yourself the following questions to clarify your situation:
1. Describe to yourself the situation that led to this crisis. How is this situation typical or atypical of your relationship? What happens when things get out of hand?
2. Are alcohol or other drugs involved and, if so, how do you feel they contribute to the problem?
3. What are some of the things that you say to yourself after an incident or argument? Describe some of your feelings, such as hurt, anger, loneliness, fear of being alone or losing your family, of being out of control, of not being able to talk about it, hopelessness, anxiety, remorsefulness, etc.
4. Do you and your partner agree on whether there is verbal, sexual, and/or physical abuse going on in the relationship?
5. What is the communication like between you and your partner? Have you shared your thoughts and feelings about your relationship and problems? Do you have a regular time together to talk honestly about your problems?
6. Do you think your partner knows how you feel (not think) about this/these incident(s)?
7. How did your parents resolve their problems while you were a child? Do you see any connections between their behavior and what happens in your relationship?
8. Do you have children? If so, what effects do you think your fights have on them? What would you like to tell them about the fights?
9. If you could change something about your behavior in a fight with your partner, what would it be? If you could change something about your partner's behavior in a fight, what would it be?
10. What ideally do you want changed in the relationship? What will it take to accomplish that? Counseling, alcohol treatment, men's counseling group, divorce, separation, or protection order, for example.
11. What do you think your partner is willing to do? What are you willing to do?
12. What kind of help, resources, or information do you need? Are there questions about the legal process or other issues that you want answered before you can make decisions about what to do?
13. What concerns do you have about your safety and that of your

children, now and for the future? Assess your need for crisis intervention.

14. How do you feel about prosecution and the charges against your partner? What is in your best interest (and the children's, if appropriate) and what do you want done about the charges?*
- If the police did not file charges against your spouse or partner and you want to press charges, you can complain directly to the district attorney. Look in the county or city government listings of the white pages of your telephone directory.

3. *Battered Women and Self-defense*

Courts are currently ruling on a battered woman's right to self-defense. Many women who have killed in self-defense are serving long-term sentences, although some have been acquitted, as was Karen Straw (p. 10).

>> In many states, to prove self-defense, the battered woman defendant must show that she had a reasonable apprehension of immediate danger of great bodily harm.

>> But courts' acceptance of the self-defense plea is not universal. A key element in many recent cases is whether or not the woman who committed the crime suffered from the "battered-woman syndrome," which refers to a set of emotional patterns and behaviors that characterize women suffering from repeated abuse.

Sometimes children who are the victims of abuse will fight back too. Two recent cases in New York have focused on teenaged women who killed their fathers, who had sexually abused them. Even though the court believed that Cheryl Pierson had been sexually abused by her father since age eleven, a New York State Supreme Court justice sentenced the eighteen-year-old to six months in jail for her role in planning her father's murder with a high school classmate. The judge, noting that he had received more than a hundred letters sympathetic to her but none condoning her actions, said that he hoped the publicity generated by the case "may produce benefit for other victims and make them aware of agencies"† to help them.

* Adapted from "Dealing with Domestic Violence," Community Mediation Program of OUR TOWN Family Center, Tuscon, Arizona, 1986. Used by permission.
†*The New York Times*, October 6, 1987.

4. Options for the Batterer or Defendant in a Domestic Violence Situation

>>> Retain a private attorney for legal advice or see if you qualify—based on income—for a court-appointed public defender.

>>> Contest a protection order with the court that issued the order.

>>> Seek an order of protection if you feel that you have been the victim of abuse.

>>> Ask the court for a continuance of your case in order to consider mediation or to seek counseling or other help.

>>> Negotiate with the prosecutor on charges against you.

>>> Seek mediation to resolve conflict with your spouse or partner; violence itself should never be mediated. *Be certain* that you *and* your partner understand the guidelines for use of mediation in a domestic violence situation on pages 15–16.

>>> Seek counseling or other help. As many as 200 programs nationwide now exclusively or as part of their work offer services to men who batter. (See Resources section.) Typically, along with counseling, these programs include crisis intervention, education, and training. Some are independent organizations run by men, which maintain close ties to battered women's shelters; others operate as adjuncts to shelters; still others offer services to men who batter as part of an interrelated, communitywide attempt to end domestic violence; a smaller number have been started by traditional mental health agencies. Although many programs for men who batter rely almost totally on volunteers and donations, others are supported by city, state, or private funds.

5. Questions and Answers on Domestic Violence, the Law, and You, the Victim of Domestic Violence*

>>> *Should I call the police?*
Yes. Domestic violence is a crime, and the police must respond to your calls no matter how many times you call them. Calling the police for assistance does not mean that you must also take further legal action, such as filing criminal charges or seeking a civil protec-

---
* See *Domestic Violence: The Law and You.*

tive order. Be sure to get the assisting officer's name and badge number.

>>> *What is the difference between civil and criminal remedies for domestic violence?*
In a civil action you are asking the court to resolve a conflict between you and the person abusing you. You are not asking the court to punish that person for breaking the law. One of the options available to you in a civil action is to seek an order of protection, also called a civil restraining order. (See pages 12–13.) A criminal complaint involves charging your attacker with a crime. Once a criminal complaint has been filed, the person charged can be arrested. A criminal charge may result in your attacker being jailed and having a criminal record.

In New York, for example, victims of domestic violence can file a complaint against their attackers in either a family court or a criminal court. Although both courts can issue an order of protection, the criminal court will prosecute the attacker for a crime. A criminal charge must be filed, and, if there is a conviction, the court may decide on a jail sentence or order the offender into counseling. The family court's purpose is to stop the violence, end family disruption, and protect the victims and their families. The judge also may order counseling or attendance in an educational program, but the attacker will not face arrest, prosecution, or a possible jail term. Both courts can also order child custody and support, and require the defendant to pay lawyer fees and any expense incurred in obtaining or enforcing an order of protection.

>>> *Should I file criminal charges?*
You will have to make up your own mind about pressing serious criminal charges. Remember that you have been the victim of a criminal act—an act not permitted between any two persons regardless of their relationship to each other. Also, remember that your failing to act may place you and your children in serious danger.

>>> *If I pursue criminal charges, what happens before the batterer's trial?*
After you have filed criminal charges, your attacker will probably be released from custody on bail or on his own word. The court that releases your attacker on bail may require him to follow certain rules, such as requiring the defendant (your attacker) not to have any contact with you. The judge who releases the defendant may allow him to return home to pick up his personal belongings. If so, ask the

judge to limit the time the defendant can stay and ask that police supervision be provided. You are entitled to get a copy of the bail order from the court clerk when you request it. Keep it in a safe place. You may need it if the defendant does not obey the bail order.

>>> *What happens if the bail order, or a sentencing order as discussed below, is not obeyed?*
Your attacker can be arrested and put in jail. Call the police immediately as you would for a violation of an order of protection. Have your copy of the order ready to show the police.

>>> *What about the defendant's trial and sentencing?*
A court hearing will be scheduled as soon as possible on your charges and you will have to testify. If the defendant is found guilty of the charges against him, he will be sentenced by the judge, who will issue a sentencing order. A copy of the sentencing order must be given to you. Keep it in a safe place. You may need to show it to the police if the defendant does not obey it.

>>> *Do I need a lawyer to pursue legal remedies against domestic violence?*
A number of states have written anti-domestic violence legislation so that a battered woman can do everything necessary on her own to seek legal redress. However, the law in this area remains somewhat complex, so you may want to consult a lawyer. Here are some suggestions for finding a lawyer, or a mediator if you want a mediator's help in resolving family conflicts. *Important:* See the discussion on the use of mediation on pages 15–16.

FINDING AN ATTORNEY

>>> Ask friends or relatives who have dealt with lawyers in a family law or general law practice for referrals; they are aware of *your* needs as well as able to comment on a particular lawyer's competence.

>>> Ask for a recommendation from a lawyer that you have used on other matters in the past and liked; a lawyer's reputation among other lawyers is a reliable indicator of that lawyer's ability.

>>> Check the referral services of your state and local bar associations for lawyers in a family law or general law practice. Telephone numbers are in the white pages of your telephone directory.

>>> Check the yellow pages for lawyers who advertise as family law, divorce, or matrimonial specialists.

>>> Ask at a women's center for referrals.

>>> Based on your income, you may be eligible for free legal assistance from a Legal Services program. Check the white pages of your telephone directory for a listing. A Legal Services lawyer or paralegal may help you obtain a temporary restraining order, testify in court, and/or deal with issues of divorce, support, custody, and visitation.

>>> Obtaining a lawyer's name by any of the methods listed above does not guarantee the lawyer's competence. You must evaluate a lawyer you are considering by using your own intuitive reaction to that person in an initial consultation interview. During the interview, determine the following:
- Does this lawyer have experience in your locality with your type of case involving domestic violence?
- How does his or her fee compare with that of other lawyers? Get a statement of the lawyer's fees *in writing*.
- How available is the lawyer for telephone calls and conferences?
- To what extent does the lawyer consult with his or her clients in making decisions related to their cases?

FINDING A MEDIATOR

>>> Ask clergy, attorneys, psychologists, and social workers if they can recommend a mediator; check with friends and relatives who have used a mediator.

>>> Check the yellow pages under "Mediation Services" for listings.

>>> Check the white pages for a state council on divorce mediation, and call for names of mediators in your area.

>>> Contact your local or state bar association for names of attorneys who act as mediators. Telephone numbers are in the white pages.

>>> Obtaining a mediator's name by any of the methods listed above does not guarantee the mediator's competence. You must evaluate a mediator you are considering by using your own intuitive reaction to that person in an initial consultation interview. During the interview, determine the following:
- How long has he or she been involved in mediation?
- How many family dispute cases has the mediator successfully mediated?
- What is the mediator's training, either past or ongoing?

- What are the mediator's fees, and how long does the mediator estimate that it will take to mediate your case? Get a statement of the mediator's fees *in writing*.
- Of what professional associations is the mediator a member?
- Can the mediator refer you to a previous client for a recommendation?
- Please carefully review the guidelines for use of mediation in an abusive relationship on pages 15–16. A mediator should not suggest or condone mediating violence.

>>> What can a battered woman do with regard to evidence to support her case? Whatever course of action you decide to take, it is *extremely* important for you to collect as much evidence of the violence as possible. Such evidence should include photographs of injuries, torn clothing, broken furnishings, and medical records. This evidence should be kept in a secure place.

6. Description of Steps and Other Definitions in the Law on Domestic Violence*

>>> *Incident:* The abuser throws objects, pushes, hits, slaps, etc. See definitions of sexual and domestic violence on pages 4–5.

>>> *Arrest of the batterer in a domestic violence situation:* The arrest will be accompanied by a charge of criminal trespass, assault, criminal damage, disturbing the peace, or disorderly conduct.

>>> *Domestic violence booking at the police station:* The abuser will usually be held in custody for eight to twenty-four hours.

>>> *The batterer's initial appearance in court:* The public defender will give counsel to the defendant, and a plea of guilty or not guilty will be entered. Then the defendant will probably be released until trial on his own word (on his "own recognizance") after bail has been set stating the conditions of his release. (See pages 21–22.)

>>> *The defendant's pre-trial appearance:* The defendant will meet with the prosecutor representing the state and you; a trial date will be set; the defendant's counsel will exchange information with the prosecutor; and the defendant might at this time change his plea.

---

* Information in this section may vary according to local and state statutes and procedures.

>>> *Trial:* The trial before a judge or jury will result in a guilty or not guilty verdict. If the defendant is found guilty, he may be sentenced to prison or probation, and/or fined.

>>> *Misdemeanor:* Criminal charge of a generally minor nature; includes simple assault, disorderly conduct, trespassing, criminal damage, malicious mischief, disturbing the peace, shoplifting, etc.

>>> *Felony:* Criminal charge of a more serious nature; includes homicide, burglary, theft, robbery, aggravated assault, manslaughter, violation of a court order, embezzlement, etc.

>>> *Probation:* Term of sentencing that grants provisional freedom on the basis of the defendant's good behavior. May be supervised or unsupervised. May include counseling or community service as a condition.

>>> *Domestic violence:* Misdemeanor criminal offense that occurs between people who are married, were formerly married, or are related by some degree of consanguinity. Some statutes include partners living together, with children.

>>> *Dismissed with prejudice:* A case is dismissed and cannot be reopened.

>>> *Dismissed without prejudice:* Case is dismissed but can be reopened within a certain period after the incident. No judgment has yet been entered.

7. Abuse of Older People and the Disabled*

The problems of older people can frequently lead to family conflict. The aging, too, can sometimes be the victims of physical assault and verbal and psychological abuse, as well as neglect, overmedication, and financial abuse. Their caretakers are most likely to be daughters and daughters-in-law, who are expected to assume the caretaking role without adequate support. These women may be caring for dependent children at the same time. Stress is high in this situation for both young and old.

Neglect and abuse of older people is a form of domestic violence that has only recently caught the attention of victims' advocates,

---

* Based on Margaret F. Hudson and Tanya F. Johnson, "A Critical Review of Research on Elder Neglect and Abuse," *The Annual Review of Gerontology and Geriatrics* 6, 1986.

researchers, and politicians. It is usually inflicted by relatives in a caregiving role on functionally impaired—physically and/or mentally—women over seventy-five years of age who cannot fully care for themselves.

In 1981 the House Select Committee on Aging estimated that one million, or 4 percent, of our older population are abused by relatives, but only one of every six cases of elder abuse comes to the attention of the authorities. Little legislation protects the frail older adult. Furthermore, the prevailing stereotype that a family protects its own members, and thus abuse of older people could not be occurring, tends to hamper this problem's recognition and remedy, as it has with other forms of family violence.

The legal rights of older people can be complex and problematic, as are issues of guardianship, criminal action, and alternatives to family care for older people.* To whom does the older person turn when relatives commit neglect and abuse? What are valid indicators of the need for guardianship? Does an older person have the right to remain in an abusive relationship?

Workers in this field have found that three models can be effective in cases of domestic violence directed against older people: the child abuse model, the domestic violence model, and the advocacy model. But much remains to be done to combat this problem. Some current options for the protection and prevention of neglect and abuse of older people are as follows:

» Institutionalize the abused older person. This is the most typical form of protection and prevention.
» Some abused older people will refuse assistance, which raises significant pastoral care and moral and legal issues.
» Seek help from community agencies, such as in-home services and counseling for the older person and his or her family, with adequate follow-up.
» Use the legal remedies outlined in this guide as models from which to extrapolate. You may want to consult an attorney, following the suggestions on pages 22–23, or there may be a Legal Services office in your area that offers services for older people with little income. See the white pages of your tele-

---

* See Mary S. Winters, "Congregational and Individual Advocacy on Aging," chapter 13, in *Older Adult Ministry: A Resource for Program Development* (Atlanta: Presbyterian Publishing House, 1987).

phone directory under "Legal Services." Abuse of the disabled is not confined to older handicapped people, however. The disabled of any age can be subject to the same physical and psychological abuse that the aging and other victims experience. Much of the above on legal rights and options for protection and prevention of abuse applies to disabled people as well.

B. SEXUAL VIOLENCE AGAINST ADULTS: RAPE

1. *Introduction**

Rape is the use of threats or violence to force a person to engage in sexual activity against her will. Rape is wrong, whatever its context: "date rape," marital rape, stranger or acquaintance rape. Today in most states rape laws are sex-neutral, allowing both men and women to prosecute or be charged with rape. Many states have abandoned the requirement that a rape victim prove that she resisted the attack "to the utmost," and that she did not consent to the intercourse. Many states, however, have retained some reference to the victim's resistance. Most states have removed the need for any corroboration of the rape besides the testimony of the victim herself. Unfortunately, prosecutors say that "rape shield" laws, which were intended to protect victims from the freewheeling inquiries into their previous sexual encounters that once characterized rape trials, afford no protection when the victim knew her assailant, even as a casual acquaintance with whom she never had sex.

Until recently there was no such crime as a husband's forced sexual intercourse with his wife. But now nearly twenty states, including New York, New Jersey, Connecticut, Florida, Wisconsin, and California, have abolished the marital exemption in some or all cases. These new rulings have been hailed as an important step in ending violence against women.

Rape statutes also legislate against sexual intercourse with victims whom the laws view as incapable of giving valid consent, such as people who are under age, mentally defective, unconscious, under the influence of alcohol or drugs, or physically helpless.

---

* Based on NOW and Cherow-O'Leary, *The State-by-State Guide,* pp. 79–83.

Statutory rape is the rape of a person who is younger than a certain age. In most states the statutory age is between ages twelve and sixteen. Before that age a person cannot give a legally valid consent to sexual intercourse.

2. *Options for the Rape Victim*

A rape victim should be examined by a doctor as soon as possible, both for her own protection and because the findings may be needed as evidence if there is a trial. As much as you may want to do so, do not shower, but go directly to a hospital emergency room or police station.

» To help overcome the emotional trauma of rape, rape crisis centers have been established nationwide to advise and comfort rape victims and to offer help through the legal process and trial.

- Most rape crisis centers have twenty-four-hour hot lines or answering services. To obtain the number, look under "rape" or "crisis" in the white pages of your telephone directory, or ask the information operator for assistance. If you cannot locate a nearby rape crisis center by these methods, call your local police precinct office (see page 12), or your local hospital and ask them. If your area does not have a center, the National Organization for Victim Assistance (NOVA), (202) 393-6682, and the National Coalition Against Sexual Assault, (618) 398-7764, will try to find one for you. If you want to speak to someone right away, contact a nearby hospital and ask for a social worker or psychiatrist on call.
- If you call a center immediately after the attack, you should inquire about what to expect if you go to a local hospital. Ask what tests will be performed; you should be examined for physical injury, sexually transmitted diseases, and pregnancy. Most crisis centers will urge you to have a medical examination that can later be used in prosecuting your attacker.
- Once a rape crisis center helps you with the medical and legal issues involved, rape trauma syndrome will be the next topic. You can decide either to have further counseling, which at a crisis center will probably be several

sessions, or be referred to a therapist for more long-term treatment.*
》 To bring criminal charges against the attacker, report the rape to the police or go directly to the district attorney's office. See page 12 on how to call the police. Look in the county or city government listings in the white pages of your telephone directory for the number of the district attorney's office. Although most states no longer have required time periods for reporting a rape, a few still require that rapes be reported within three to six months.
》 A rape victim can consider suing the rapist for damages in a civil action. A majority of states allow these suits. Consult an attorney for details.
》 A rape victim can consider suing a third person other than the attacker for damages in a civil action. Many jurisdictions permit suits against landlords and owners of hotels and supermarkets who may have contributed to the occurrence through lax security practices. Check with an attorney about your state's policies.

3. *Options for the Accused Rapist*

》》 Retain a private attorney for legal advice, or see if you qualify—based on income—for a court-appointed public defender.
》》 Negotiate with the prosecutor on charges against you.
》》 Obtain counseling.

4. *Questions and Answers on Sexual Assault, the Law, and You, the Victim of Sexual Assault*†

》》 *As a victim of sexual assault, do I need a lawyer?*
No. Under our system of laws, a crime is considered to be an offense against society, so it is the prosecuting attorney, or lawyer for the county or city, who prosecutes the accused person. The prosecuting attorney represents your interests because the victim is the most important witness for the prosecution.

---

* See "Psychological Effects of Rape," *Glamour,* August 1987, p. 184.
† Based on Sexual Assault Center, Harborview Medical Center, *The Victim of Sexual Assault and the Law* (Seattle, 1987).

>>> *What else must I do to assist in prosecuting the case against my attacker?*
It is almost always necessary for the victim of sexual assault to be interviewed by the police and the prosecutor's office staff. You are a crucial part of the prosecution process and have a right to know what is happening and why. Do not be afraid to ask questions or to ask for assistance in dealing with the various aspects of the criminal justice system.

>>> *What else should I know about prosecution of the offender?*
The defendant's lawyer is called a defense attorney, and his or her job is to represent the interests of the offender, not those of you, the victim. *Do not* discuss the case with the defense attorney unless the prosecuting attorney is present. If the defense attorney requests an interview with you, it should be arranged through the prosecutor's office. You have a right to have this interview in the presence of a prosecutor and an advocate—someone who helps victims through the legal system by offering support and information.

>>> *Will my attacker be able to "plea bargain" on the charges against him?*
Probably. Between the time that charges are filed and the trial date, the defense attorney and the prosecuting attorney may make an agreement that the defendant will plead guilty to all the charges in return for a specific sentence recommendation, plead guilty to one of several charges, or plead guilty to a lesser offense. You should be consulted about the prosecutor's recommendation, and can give your opinion.

>>> *What can I expect before and during my attacker's trial?*
There is a trial only if the defendant is pleading not guilty to having committed the offense. The prosecuting attorney then has to prove the charges to the jury or judge beyond a reasonable doubt. The prosecuting attorney will contact you before the trial and review the questions that will be asked, explain court procedures, and prepare you for testifying in court. The victim must testify, and be cross-examined by the defense attorney. The defendant may or may not testify, but must be in court. If the defendant is found guilty, you do not have to be at the sentencing, but you are encouraged to be present, and to write a letter to the judge explaining in detail how this experience affected you and your family and what you would recommend for sentencing.

C. SEXUAL HARASSMENT IN THE WORKPLACE*

Sexual harassment is an unlawful employment practice under Title VII of the Civil Rights Act of 1964. The Equal Employment Opportunity Commission's "Guidelines on Discrimination Because of Sex" define this behavior as "unwelcome sexual advances, requests for sexual favors, and other verbal or physical conduct of a sexual nature when submission to such conduct is either explicitly or implicitly a term or condition of an individual's employment." You need not lose specific job benefits to state a claim; it is sufficient if your ability to function effectively and productively at work is interfered with. Various studies of harassment have shown that nearly half of all working women have been harassed at some point.

Probably the most important advice for a victim of sexual harassment is that adequate documentation is important to substantiate claims.

Options for the sexual harassment victim are as follows:

» First, say no in very clear language to unwelcome sexual advances.

» If verbal refusal does not work, inform you company's management in writing of the problem, and state that this behavior is a violation of Title VII. Keep a copy of all correspondence to and from management.

» File charges with the Equal Employment Opportunity Commission in your area. The telephone number is in the white pages of your telephone directory under the U.S. government listings. As with other Title VII claims, strict time limits must be observed in the filing of a complaint.

» State law remedies may also assist the victim of sexual harassment. In many states, for example, women can bring civil tort actions for assault, intentional infliction of emotional distress, tortious interference with business relations, or wrongful discharge. Consult with an attorney in your area.

---

* See NOW and Cherow-O'Leary, *The State-by-State Guide*, pp. 65–66.

» III «
Domestic and Sexual Violence Against Children

A. CHILD ABUSE

1. Introduction

Factors that contribute to a parent abusing his or her child include immaturity, unrealistic expectations of children, lack of parenting knowledge, social isolation, unmet emotional needs of the parent, and the parent having had experience of abuse and/or emotional deprivation as a child. As with other forms of family violence, wealth, status, education, and religion offer no protection against child abuse. Major or minor crises, usually recurring crises, and alcohol or drug abuse may trigger it.

2. Definitions of Child Abuse

>>> *Physical abuse* is shaking, beating, burning, depriving the child of necessities, slapping, kicking, pushing, hard squeezing, etc.

>>> *Verbal abuse* is excessive yelling, belittling, cruel teasing, etc. Words can hit as hard as a fist: "You're pathetic. You can't do anything right!" "You disgust me! Just shut up!" "Why don't you go and find some other place to live. I wish you'd never been born!"

>>> *Emotional abuse* is coldness; withdrawal; failure to provide loving attention, supervision, or normal living experiences.

>>> *Sexual abuse* is incest, rape, or any other sexual intrusion into the child's physical and/or mental integrity. (See next section.)

3. Typical State Statute Prohibiting Child Abuse

The nurturing and upbringing of children have traditionally been the right and responsibility of the family. However, if a family is unable or unwilling to carry out this role, the community must intervene for the protection of the child. New York's statute prohibiting child abuse is characteristic of such state statutes and provides that

> Harm or threatened harm to a child's physical or mental health or welfare by the acts or omissions of the parent or other person responsible for the child's welfare, if the child is under 18, is prohibited. Harm and threatened harm include physical or mental injury inflicted by other than accidental means; sexual offenses against a child; neglect; abandonment; or failure to provide adequate food, clothing, shelter, health care and education.*

New York's Social Services Law establishes a New York State central register of child abuse and maltreatment as well as a central registry in New York City. Reports may be made by telephone or in writing, and are kept confidential. Your city or state may have a similar registry for reports of child abuse. If you seriously suspect child abuse, check in the white pages of your telephone directory under the listings for your state and/or city government's department of social services.

4. Options in a Child Abuse Situation

>>> *Victim.* Seek help outside your family from a teacher, minister, counselor, friend's parents, doctor, or anyone you trust. *Don't be afraid* to reach out. You may have to reach out to more than one person.

>>> *Abusive parent.* Every parent shares the feelings of acute irritation, frustration, and stress that lie behind the actions of those who are violently cruel to their children, but parents are responsible for finding ways to deal with their frustration without harming their children. If you cannot deal with your frustrations and have abused your child, ask for help *now*. You can start by calling Parents Anonymous' toll-free number: 1-800-421-0353. You can use this number as a hot line in case of crisis as well as for referrals to resources for help. Check the white pages of your telephone directory for local hot lines under "child abuse," and in the listings for your state, county, and/or city government's social services department. Or dial "0" (zero, not "o") on your telephone, or your area's directory assistance to get the number of a parents' helpline.

* Fam. Ct. Act 1012.

>>> *Person aware of child abuse.* If possible, offer your help in getting help to the parent and/or child. Or if you are reasonably certain that child abuse exists, you may report the abuse. In some states, reporting is mandatory, and in others, reporting is merely encouraged. Some people reject mandatory reporting and intervention in cases of family violence on the following grounds:
- Mandatory reporting is seen as punitive rather than as protective.
- Our system of laws may shift the victim's self-determination and autonomy to impersonal authorities, although this is not a valid consideration in the case of child abuse.
- A mandatory reporting system emphasizes the label of family deviance and the prognosis of family deterioration, some researchers have stated.*

In the case of child abuse, however, it is clear that protecting the child must be the first priority when deciding to report suspected abuse. You may be someone who *must* report child abuse; check the information above on mandatory reporting and your state's statute. Making a report in good faith—to the best of your knowledge and without malicious intent—protects you from legal liability.

People who abuse children or other family members, either physically or sexually, need help. They need to be held accountable for their actions, and to learn new ways of interacting that are not damaging. Providing the kind of help that they need is complicated. Abusers often deny and minimize harm, and project responsibility for it onto the victim. Counseling abusers is a job for professionals. Whether you are a pastor or a layperson, *do not* attempt yourself to counsel an abuser. Unless you are a specialist in this field you may do additional harm. Urge and help abusers who speak to you about their problem to find a reputable treatment program and *stick with it.* Pastors in particular may be approached by abusers for confession and forgiveness. Always stress that forgiveness is not a substitute for counseling by an experienced professional. Always be aware of the disposition of abusers to manipulate others into sharing their view of the abuse. Naiveté about abusers is dangerous. Make sure, for example, that you do not tell an abuser that the victim spoke with

---

* See Margaret F. Hudson and Tanya F. Johnson, "A Critical Review of Research on Elder Neglect and Abuse," *The Annual Review of Gerontology and Geriatrics* 6, 1986.

you about the abuse—the abuser may retaliate by further abusing the victim.

If a minor speaks to you about physical or sexual abuse by a family member, tell the child that you are obligated to report it: "We want the abuse to stop, but we can't do it alone. We need help." Do not make promises to children that you cannot keep. Assure children that you will stand by them during investigations and any court proceedings that may follow. If they are removed to a foster home—despite many problems, this is often the best means of ensuring their safety—your continued contact can be deeply important. Do not abandon such children.*

5. The Case Against Spanking Children

What are we teaching our children when we resort to physical or verbal violence against them? One father commented, "I'm sure that my inability to control my temper is the biggest factor in our kids' learning violence."† Researchers have observed the following effects of regular spanking:

- » Children who are often spanked tend to be quieter, less articulate, and more sullen, even becoming chronically passive.
- » Spanking tends to create nervousness and skittishness, and to slow down learning and interest in learning.
- » Harsh physical and psychological punishment leads to emotional distance among family members, anger and loss of love, and a deterioration in communication. Resentment, hurt, and anger felt by an abused child may last his or her lifetime.
- » Violence begets violence. Physical punishment for fighting cannot teach children to seek nonviolent solutions to conflict. If spanking does not work to control an unwanted behavior, some parents fall into the trap of escalating the spanking until a child is permanently injured, either physically or psychologically, or killed.
- » Children who are controlled through being spanked can develop a dangerous overdependence on external controls.

---

* Based on Division for Parish Services, Lutheran Church in America, "Ministry to Abusive Families," from the Family Resources series.
† Kathleen McGinnis and James McGinnis, *Parenting for Peace and Justice* (Maryknoll, NY: Orbis Books, 1981), p. 39.

Parents, lawmakers, and educators are currently challenging the longstanding authority of public school officials in forty-one states to administer corporal punishment, based on a growing perception that corporal punishment can be child abuse.*

》 A ten-year study showed that even students who did not show lasting physical damage were often the victims of emotional scars that produced nightmares and vomiting.

》 Corporal punishment is used disproportionately on poor black, Hispanic, and emotionally troubled students, particularly males.

》 Corporal punishment does not improve educational performance, but rather fuels a cycle of violence among its young victims. Paddling has been shown to have little deterrent effect because it is the same students who are paddled repeatedly.

》 "Good" children also worry about getting paddled, which saps their energy for learning.

B. SEXUAL ABUSE OF CHILDREN†

1. *Definitions*

》》 Sexual abuse of children (also called child molesting) may be *nonphysical:* indecent exposure, obscene telephone calls, peeping toms, or child pornography.

》》 *Physical sexual abuse* is genital or oral stimulation, fondling, or sexual intercourse, including incest and rape. Incest is sexual activity, intimate physical contact that is sexually arousing, between family members who are not partners.

2. *What You Can Do*

》》 Help prevent child sexual abuse by providing children with clear, accurate information about sexual abuse. Teach children how to protect themselves. Encourage children to tell you about any incidents. Report even suspected cases to the authorities.

* *The New York Times*, July 9, 1987.
† Based on "What Everyone Should Know About the Sexual Abuse of Children" (South Deerfield, MA: Channing L. Bete Co., 1983).

>>> If you learn that a child has been sexually abused, immediately contact the appropriate social agency and the police. Making a report in good faith protects you from legal liability.
- Agencies that can help in cases of child sexual abuse include child abuse centers and the child welfare or child protective services of your city's or county's department of social services. Check in the white pages of your telephone directory under the city or county government listings. These agencies can give psychological counseling and other help to the victim and his or her family.
- The police should be informed about physical aggression or strange behavior toward a child as well as actual incidents of sexual abuse. This might help to prevent harm to other children. Report all the details that you can, even those that seem unimportant.

>>> If you learn that a child has been sexually abused, also do the following:
- Believe the child, no matter how hard it is. Children seldom lie about sexual abuse. Even if the child fabricated the incident, help is needed for the child in any event.
- Try to control your own emotions. Fear and anger are normal reactions but can further frighten the child. Let the child know that your feelings are not directed at him or her. Never blame, punish, or embarrass the child.
- Give emotional support to the child. Give reassurance that he or she is safe and that no harm will come from reporting the incident. Let the child ask questions. Give answers in terms he or she can understand.
- Get information. Find out as much as possible about the events leading up to, during, and after the incident. If the abuser was a stranger, try to get a description of physical features, clothing, car, etc.
- Get medical assistance. Promptly contact a physician for treatment of physical injuries. Ask the physician or other health worker to refer you to a counselor experienced in dealing with this type of problem.

>>> If you formally file a complaint with the police about an incident of sexual abuse of a child that results in an arrest, the legal process for prosecuting the child's attacker will be similar to that described for a

rape prosecution. (See pages 29–30.) The child may be called to testify in court, or may be interviewed in the judge's chambers or on videotape, or the child may not be asked to testify about the incident, based on the court's evaluation of the danger of traumatizing the child by forcing him or her to relive the incident. The child's family and/or therapist can help the judge to make that decision.

>>> See the suggestions for a person aware of child abuse on pages 34–35.

» IV «
How Church Members and Ministers Can Work Against Violence in Our Society

A. Work Against Bias Against Women in the Court System

In courtrooms nationwide many women still find that their legal claims and credibility or character are being judged on the basis of factors that seem, to many legal experts and victims' advocates, to be antiquated, irrelevant, and prejudicial: the company they keep, their sexual mores, and how they walk, talk, dress, and handle their emotions. Legal experts and social scientists say that this is often true whether the issue is custody, sexual assault, domestic violence, the division of marital property, or the awarding of damages in wrongful death suits. The New York Task Force on Women in the Courts, a twenty-three-member panel, issued a report in 1986 that concluded after an eighteen-month study that sex bias in the court system was "pervasive." This finding could almost certainly apply to other states.

Here are some suggestions for countering this unjust situation:
» Speak out in whatever contexts are available to you on the wrongfulness of victims of crimes of sexual assault and other violence having to prove their own innocence.
» Encourage the growing willingness of state court officials to recognize that the problem of systemic bias against women exists, and to work toward eradicating it.
» Make sure that your local and state bar association is working to sensitize members to the problem.
» Support efforts to make sex bias a prominent part of law school curriculums.

B. Develop Helping Relationships with Both the Abused and the Abuser*

>>> Understand the abused partner's problems from her perspective. Actively listen by asking questions and helping to make connections so that the victim can clarify her feelings and thoughts. Gently but firmly confront the victim's inappropriate guilt feelings and sense of responsibility for her partner's abusive behavior.

>>> Understand the abusive partner's problems from his perspective. Be as empathetic and responsive with the abusive partner as with the abused partner, but do not condone violent and abusive behavior. Avoid judgments or criticism as you gain information about specific situations and abusive behaviors.

>>> Reinforce both partners' efforts to do something about the violence. Acknowledge the difficulty they may be experiencing in speaking with you as a member of the clergy or as a concerned layperson about their problems. Emphasize that they may have already applied some skills in attempting to solve the problem that can be built on. Help the partners to understand the consequences of not reaching out for help—the problem of family violence will not go away by itself.

>>> Explain to them what community resources might be available to them to help. Offer them this guide as a resource, and offer your assistance in making initial telephone calls.

C. What New York State Has Done: Suggestions for Lobbying Initiatives

Get together with other groups in your area to form a coalition, or join a group already established to lobby for the following and other measures on family violence. And/or write, call, or visit your legislators on your own to urge their support. You may want to initiate the following actions in your own state:
   >> A law to allow victims of household violence, including not only spouses but also former spouses and live-in partners with

---

* Based on David Harvey (Counseling and Consulting Services, Tucson, AZ, 1986) in "Dealing with Domestic Violence."

a common child, to make a complaint against their attackers in either a family court or a criminal court, depending on the remedies sought.
» Establishment of a Children and Family Trust Fund. In New York this trust fund receives state monies as well as contributions to provide grants for programs and services that combat family violence and prevent child abuse. An advisory board directs the funding, establishment, and evaluation of such programs.
» A much-needed service when family violence occurs is emergency housing for victims and their children. A legislative initiative to provide seed money has resulted in more than fifteen shelters for victims in New York and more than 200 service programs that provide counseling and legal assistance.
» Lobby for a government-funded hot line in your state if one is not available. It can provide crisis intervention, counseling, and information.
» Initiate a measure that requires police officers investigating a family offense to provide the victim with information on appropriate community services.
» New York has also been active in correcting past injustices that have affected victims of sexual abuse in ways that other states might want to consider implementing. With the repeal of the requirement for corroborating evidence before a jury could consider a rape or incest case, victims' rights have been further ensured. A recent law also removed the need for a young victim to have corroborating testimony in many cases.
» Recognizing that rape is a trauma that can cause financial burdens, the New York state senate approved a measure that entitles a rape victim to be reimbursed by the state Crime Victims Board (CVB) for expenses for a hospital or medical examination connected with the investigation or prosecution of a sexual offense. The CVB also reimburses a rape victim for lost wages owing to an assault. To be compensated, a woman must report the rape to the police within one week.

Like other states—although perhaps not yet your state—New York prohibits a defendant from introducing evidence of the rape victim's past sexual conduct unless it is directly relevant to the case; does not demand evidence that a rape victim "earnestly resisted" her attacker; and allows married men to be prosecuted for raping their wives, whether they are legally separated or not.

D. *Advocate Within the Church Against Sexual and Domestic Violence*

⟫⟫ Observe National Domestic Violence Week during October. Contact the Center for the Prevention of Sexual and Domestic Violence or the National Coalition Against Domestic Violence for more information. (See Resources section.)

⟫⟫ Many victims benefit from support groups, both for those who have left a battering relationship and for those who have chosen to remain. Offer your church building as a space for such groups to meet. Be sure to make provisions for child care.

⟫⟫ Encourage your minister or a committed layperson to seek training in how to respond to a victim of physical or sexual abuse, or to an abuser. Familiarity with this guide is a good beginning, although clergy and concerned laity should be certain that they also know their own state's laws against sexual and domestic violence. But be aware that only a trained specialist should attempt long-term counseling of an abused person and, in particular, an abuser.

⟫⟫ Place posters advertising services for victims of sexual and domestic violence in your community. Have brochures on these services available in the narthex. Include information about services or programs in your church newsletter.

⟫⟫ Encourage church members to volunteer for the local shelter or rape crisis line. Include these local programs in the mission budget of the church or in the giving of the women's group.

⟫⟫ Participate in providing shelter through a safe home network in your community.

⟫⟫ Be prepared and sensitive in responding to the abused woman in your midst. Remember that the abuse or assault is not her fault. She needs your caring support, prayers, and possibly financial support.

⟫⟫ Preach about and against family and sexual violence from the pulpit. This can help to prevent domestic and sexual violence and to encourage victims to tell what happened to them.

⟫⟫ Offer an adult study series on family and sexual violence. Invite prosecutors and representatives from local shelters and rape crisis groups to speak. Conduct Bible study on women and violence.

⟫⟫ Programs for teens may be especially important. For many, the teen years may be the time when young men learn the stereotypes that to be manly is to be tough and in control, and when young women learn that to be feminine means to be nonassertive. Sexual assault and battering among teenage couples are being recognized as serious problems. Confirmation classes, youth meetings, and teen church school classes can be important places for prevention programs. Use Marie Fortune's curriculum on violence (see Resource section). The teen years are also times when child victims of family abuse struggle desperately to get free. Centers for runaways, teen prostitutes, and chemically dependent teens testify to the massive numbers who have been victims of incest or physical abuse. Support these services in your community.

⟫⟫ Marriage ceremonies and premarital counseling can be important symbolic occasions for theological messages against family violence. Clergy may make a habit of including questions about conflict resolution and the inappropriate use of force in premarital counseling. Consider suggesting biblical readings at weddings that comment on peace rather than on the submission of women or traditional sex-role stereotypes.

E. Work Within the Church Against Child Abuse and Sexual Assault

⟫⟫ Talk about and study the issue to raise awareness of child abuse and sexual assault.

⟫⟫ Provide programs to help parents understand themselves and their children's needs and development, and how to improve their parenting skills. Contact the Human Development Office, United Church Board for Homeland Ministries, for a resource list (see Resource section).

⟫⟫ Provide training for recognizing the signs of child abuse and sexual assault, and reporting it, especially for church school and day-care teachers.

>>> Include the issues in marriage preparation and enrichment programs.

>>> Become aware of resources in the community to help child abuse victims and their families.

>>> Support efforts of social agencies and police to deal with the problems of child abuse and sexual assault.

>>> Encourage and support specialized treatment for the abuser and the child when incest is involved.

>>> Encourage treatment of abusers, in or out of prison, in addition to punishment.

>>> Support children's rights to accurate information about child sexual abuse.

>>> Many resources in child sexual abuse prevention education exist today. They can be as simple as coloring books or video programs. Local rape crisis centers can make recommendations. Ask your church school to consider making a prevention program an annual event. Teaching all children the "personal safety rules"—say no, get away, tell someone—should be as basic as teaching them fire or traffic safety rules.

>>> Advocate for or support such education in your area's public schools.

>>> Familiarize yourself with this guide, although you should also be sure that you know your own state's laws against child abuse.

>>> Clergy are among "mandated" reporters of child abuse under state law, which means that they *must* report suspected abuse when they "have reason to believe that a child has suffered harm as a result of abuse or maltreatment," in the words of the typical New York statute (Soc. Serv. Sec. 420). Clergy are encouraged to consider this duty and the mechanisms for carrying it out *prior* to having to address an actual incident of child abuse.

F. *Recommendations for Preventing and Remedying Abuse of Older People**

>>> Health care professionals need better training in caring for older people, including a strong educational component on the aging

* See Margaret F. Hudson and Tanya F. Johnson, "A Critical Review of Research on Elder Neglect and Abuse," *The Annual Review of Gerontology and Geriatrics* 6, 1986.

process and cues for detecting potential and actual neglect and abuse of older people.

》》》 Professional researchers should be encouraged to devote more effort to the problem of mistreatment of older people, and the legal and legislative systems should evaluate and clarify the rights of caregivers and older people.

》》》 Physical and mental health systems should provide more effective counseling and support for families caring for an older member.

》》》 In general, we need to address and intervene in the causes rather than the symptoms of abuse of older people, as with all forms of family violence.

》》》 Establish a pool of volunteer nursing home visitors who are trained in detecting signs of abuse in older people.

G. Advocate Against Sexual and Domestic Violence in the Larger Society

In the community:
- 》 Provide court-watchers to monitor proceedings on sexual and domestic violence for fairness and for sensitivity to the victim.
- 》 Serve on boards of directors for local agencies that are working on these issues.
- 》 Testify as a concerned clergy or layperson before governmental bodies that are considering new legislation dealing with sexual and domestic violence.
- 》 Write letters to the editor of your local newspaper commending or criticizing its coverage of sexual and domestic violence.
- 》 Participate in community fund-raisers for programs dealing with sexual and domestic violence.
- 》 Pledge your financial support to local and national programs that are working to end violence against women and children.
- 》 Hot lines for abusers to call before they hurt people are becoming available in many communities. If your region has not begun such a service, consider initiating one. Organizations such as Parents Anonymous—there are branches throughout the country—welcome volunteers to staff their hot lines.

In the legal system:
- 》 Encourage your local police to consider a policy of nondiscretionary arrests in domestic violence cases, which means that a

police officer has no choice but to arrest if he or she believes violence has occurred. These programs have been effective in reducing battering. Some cities sponsor community intervention projects along with the mandatory arrest; female and male volunteers provide immediate counseling for both victims and offenders. Your good will and support may be important.

» The police also need training programs for dealing more effectively with domestic and sexual violence, including crisis intervention techniques, legal guidance for fully informing battered women of their rights, and fuller coordination with other agencies trying to protect and help victims.

» Courts should strive to cut red tape and eliminate delays in victims obtaining restraining and protective orders, peace bonds, etc.

» Legal aid programs should increase services to battered spouses who seek divorce, custody, etc.

» Stronger, more effective laws governing domestic violence are still needed in some states.

» Legislation is needed to adequately fund improvements in preventing and remedying domestic and sexual violence. Be supportive of such measures as a taxpayer and a voter.

» All court personnel—judges, lawyers, and court officers—should be trained in further sensitivity to the issues of sexual and domestic violence, and to the fact of bias against women in our court system.

» V «

Resources

A. NATIONAL TOLL-FREE HOT LINES

1. National Child Abuse Hot Line: 1-800-422-4453
   Twenty-four-hour service that will supply you with the child abuse hot line number for your area.
2. National Coalition Against Domestic Violence: 1-800-333-7233
3. Parents Anonymous: 1-800-421-0353

B. ORGANIZATIONS

1. The Center for the Prevention of Sexual and Domestic Violence
   1914 N. 34 Street
   Seattle, WA 98103
   The Rev. Marie Fortune, Executive Director
   (206) 634-1903
   The center is an interreligious, educational ministry that provides resources to the religious community and organizations in the United States and Canada in response to sexual and domestic violence.
2. Human Development Office
   Division of the American Missionary Association
   United Church Board for Homeland Ministries
   132 West 31 Street
   New York, NY 10001
   Faith A. Johnson, Secretary for Human Development
   (212) 239-8700
   Working to prevent sexual and domestic violence is an important component of the Human Development Office's focus on family life. Copies of the United Church of Christ's Pronouncement on

Violence Against Women and other resources for developing effective family life ministries are available from this office.

3. The Interfaith Conciliation Center
   199 N. Columbus Avenue
   Mount Vernon, NY 10553
   (914) 699-8554
   ICC sponsored an invitational dialogue event at the Marydale Retreat Center in Covington, KY, on October 12–14, 1986, called "Dialogue on Mediation of Family and Relational Conflicts." Ending sexual and domestic violence is an important priority for ICC.

4. The National Coalition Against Domestic Violence
   2401 Virginia Avenue, NW, Suite 305
   Washington, DC 20037
   (202) 293-8860
   National Toll-free Hot Line: 1-800-333-7233
   NCADV is a network of concerned individuals and agencies that provides training and support for local programs and legislative action at the federal level. A national directory of domestic violence programs can be ordered for $2.50 to cover postage and handling.

5. National Coalition Against Sexual Assault
   Volunteers of America
   8787 State Street, Suite 202
   East St. Louis, IL 62203
   Fern Ferguson, President
   (618) 398-7764
   Provides information, referrals, and other resources on domestic violence.

6. National Center for Missing and Exploited Children
   1835 K Street, NW, Suite 700
   Washington, DC 20006
   (202) 634-9821

7. National Council on Child Abuse and Family Violence
   Plaza La Reina
   6033 West Century Boulevard, Suite 400
   Los Angeles, CA 90045
   (818) 914-2814

(800) 222-2000
Washington, DC Office: (202) 429-6695

8. National Organization for Victim Assistance (NOVA)
717 D Street, NW, 2d Floor
Washington, DC 20004
(202) 393-NOVA

9. Rape and Violence End Now (RAVEN)
P.O. Box 24159
St. Louis, MO 63130
(314) 725-6137
RAVEN is an all-male collective that publishes *Network News*, a quarterly newsletter that covers the range of programs that address ending men's violence against women. Both men and women can join the network. RAVEN also publishes a directory of programs nationwide for batterers, which is available for $8.00, plus $2.00 for postage and handling. Bulk prices are also available.

C. PUBLICATIONS

1. Bussert, Joy M.K. *Battered Women: From a Theology of Suffering to an Ethic of Empowerment.* Division for Mission in North America, Lutheran Church in America, 1986. Contact DMNA Interpretation, 231 Madison Avenue, New York, NY 10016. $3.50 plus $1.00 postage and handling. Checks payable to Lutheran Church in America.

2. Channing L. Bete Co., Inc. "About the Sexual Abuse of Children," "About Wife Abuse," and "What Everyone Should Know About the Sexual Abuse of Children." From the Scriptographic Booklet series, which also includes "About Anger," "About Self-Esteem," and "Family Violence." Available in English and in Spanish. Order from Channing L. Bete Co., Inc., 200 State Road, South Deerfield, MA 01373. 1-800-628-7733.

3. Fortune, Marie M.
   Is Nothing Sacred? The Betrayal of the Pastoral Relationship. In press.
   Keeping the Faith: Questions and Answers for the Abused Woman. San Francisco: Harper & Row, 1987.
   Sexual Abuse Prevention: A Study for Teenagers. United Church

Press, 1984.

Sexual Violence: The Unmentionable Sin. The Pilgrim Press, 1983.

4. McGinnis, Kathleen, and James McGinnis. *Parenting for Peace and Justice.* Maryknoll, NY: Orbis Books, 1981.

5. NOW Legal Defense and Education Fund and Dr. Renée Cherow-O'Leary. *The State-by-State Guide to Women's Legal Rights.* New York: McGraw-Hill, 1987.

6. United States Catholic Conference, Office of Domestic Social Development. *Violence in the Family: A National Concern, a Church Concern.* Prepared by Barbara Ann Stolz, Publications Office, U.S. Catholic Conference, 1312 Massachusetts Avenue, NW, Washington, DC 20005, 1979.

7. Winters, Mary S. *Divorce Law: A Concise Guide for Clergy and Laity.* New York: The Pilgrim Press, 1986.

Appendix: The United Church of Christ's Pronouncement on Violence Against Women (1983)

The United Church of Christ voted at its 14th General Synod:

The Pronouncement on Violence Against Women

I. SUMMARY

As Christians, believing in the sacredness of God's creation and in the equality of women and men, we are called to speak out against the physical and/or sexual abuse of any person. Because women are the primary victims of domestic violence, rape, and sexual harassment, this Pronouncement calls for the United Church of Christ to increase its understanding of violence against women, provide ministry to victims and abusers, and work against violence in our society.

II. ORIGIN

The Thirteenth General Synod called upon the United Church Board for Homeland Ministries to draft a major pronouncement and proposals for action on Violence Against Women for the consideration of the Fourteenth General Synod, and to be in consultation with the Coordinating Center for Women, the Office for Church in Society, and the Commission for Racial Justice in preparation of the Pronouncement and proposals.

III. BACKGROUND AND RATIONALE

Violence is widespread in American homes and society. A high percentage of that violence is directed against women and children. Every five minutes a forcible rape occurs in this country.[1] Every 30 seconds a child is abused.[2] One-tenth of these cases are sexual abuse. In 85 percent of these latter cases, the abuser is a family member or acquaintance of the child.[3]

---

[1] Mary Pellauer, "Violence Against Women: The Theological Dimension," *Christianity and Crisis*, Vol 43, #9 (May 30, 1983), p. 206.
[2] *marriage and divorce today*, May 10, 1982, p. 4.
[3] Marie Fortune and Denise Hormann, "Family Violence: A Workshop Manual for

Every 60 seconds a case of physical spousal assault will be reported to the police.[4] If a woman, you have a one in six chance of being raped.[5] If a married woman, you have a one in seven chance of being raped by your husband,[6] and the law of your state may offer you no protection at all. If a married woman or if a woman cohabiting with a male, you have a one in two chance of being physically battered.[7]

This abuse goes on each hour of the day, each day of the week, each week of the year. To compound the horror, recent research suggests that today's abused will be tomorrow's abuser.[8] Thus the problem becomes generational, reminding us of the biblical phrase "The fathers have eaten sour grapes and the children's teeth are set on edge." This Pronouncement does not address violence generally in our society, does not focus on violence against women and men, and does not survey violence as the "human condition." This is by intention because women and girls of all ages are the primary victims of "domestic" or "family" violence, just as they are the primary victims of rape, sexual abuse, or sexual harassment.

"Domestic" or "family" violence includes spouse battering, child abuse or neglect, and elder abuse (which the media have christened "granny bopping" because elderly women are the most frequent victims), as well as marital rape and incest. It can even include violence carried to the extreme of murder. But whatever its kind, domestic violence injures women and children more frequently and more seriously than it does men.

Dr. Murray Straus, America's foremost authority on domestic violence, asserts that almost 30 percent of all married couples admit violent behavior.[9] Assuming that many hesitate to admit their acts, he estimates that 50–60 percent of all married couples experience serious forms of violence at some time.[10] A similar or even higher level of violence may occur among cohabiting or courting couples.[11]

Clergy and Other Service Providers," Monograph 6 (April 1981) of the Domestic Violence monograph series of the National Clearinghouse on Domestic Violence, pp. 66–67.

[4] "Myths and Facts About Rape and Battering," pamphlet, Council on Women and the Church, United Presbyterian Church in the USA.

[5] Martin and Braen, Univ. of Kentucky College of Medicine, reported in *Journal of American Medical Association*, cited in "Rape Trauma Challenging," *Seattle Times*, March 27, 1983.

[6] Diana Russell, *Rape in Marriage*, 1983.

[7] Lenore Walker, *Battered Wives*, 1979.

[8] Straus, Gelles, and Steinmetz, *Behind Closed Doors: Violence in the American Family* (Garden City, NY: Anchor Press/Doubleday, 1980).

[9] Murray Straus, Univ. of NH, "Normative and Behavioral Aspects of Violence Between Spouses," unpublished paper dated March 15, 1977.

[10] Herbert Yahraes, "Physical Violence in Families," in *families today, a research sampler on families and children*, Vol 11, National Institute of Mental Health, Science Monograph series, 1979, p. 562.

[11] "Campus Couples and Violence," *NY Times*, June 23, 1981. Based on papers given at the meeting of the Western Social Science Association, San Diego, CA.

Violent behavior in the home includes throwing things; pushing or shoving; slapping, kicking, or biting; hitting with a fist; beating; threatening with a knife or a gun; slashing or shooting. Only the last several actions are considered in Straus' statistics. It is a sad commentary on American families that many of these actions are often viewed as "normal" in families. Violent behavior also includes sexual assault, which may occur either within or outside the family unit.

Both men and women use violence, but the violent male usually does far more damage than does the violent woman.[12] Abusive men are particularly likely to attack a woman when she is pregnant, thereby intensifying the damage.[13] But individuals need not resort to constant violence: one episode can "establish the balance of power within the relationship for a lifetime."[14]

Violence in the home inflicts suffering on children and the elderly as well. Over one million cases of child abuse are reported each year; many thousands undoubtedly go unreported.[15] Two thousand children die each year from physical abuse.[16] In the home, as in society at large, over 80 percent of all victims of sexual abuse are girls.[17] With more mothers cohabiting with men who are not the fathers of their children, sexual abuse of the woman's daughters by the live-in male is increasing. But incest is also widespread, the major incestuous abuser of girls being the child's father or stepfather.[18] Finally, one million persons 65 or older are abused physically or sexually each year. Women, who outlive men, are the primary victims.[19]

Violence, power, and the lack of power are closely related. Force is socially accepted as an indicator of power, and the physically weak can easily be victimized by the physically stronger.[20] Male violence against women and children has often been seen as legitimate within families, since force demonstrates man's traditional role—often thought to be biblically based—as head of the family.

Women who remain in a violent relationship do so for many reasons, often because they themselves accept the familiar sexual stereotypes which declare that the male should be dominant and the female subordinate. Women who are economically dependent are particularly likely to accept physical, sexual, or psychological abuse from husbands or partners, par-

---

[12] Murray Straus, "Wife Beating: How Common and Why?" *Victimology*, Vol. 2, #33, 1977–78, p. 449.
[13] Yahraes, p. 570.
[14] Yahraes, p. 561.
[15] Peter Coolsen, "Community Involvement in the Prevention of Child Abuse and Neglect," *Children Today*, September/October, 1980, p. 6.
[16] Fortune and Hormann, p. 66.
[17] Figures from the Sexual Assault Center of Seattle, WA. Quoted by the Rev. Marie Fortune in "Sexual Violence," *JSAC Grapevine*, Vol. 11, #3, September, 1979.
[18] Marcia Yudkin, "Breaking the Incest Taboo," *The Progressive*, May, 1981.
[19] U.S. House Committee on Aging, 1981, in *Response*, Vol. 6, #2, March/April 1983.
[20] For discussion, see, for example, Susan Brownmiller, *Against Our Will: Men, Women, and Rape* (NY: Simon and Schuster, 1975).

ticularly if they have children dependent upon them.[21] Tragically, they may then prove that they possess at least some power by using force on their children. Abusive parents often believe that parents who spare the rod, spoil the child. In the light of the violence that flourishes within families, the myth of the home as a place of unchanging love, support, and peace needs re-examination, as do the sexual stereotypes and social inequalities which disadvantage women in their relationships with men.

The cultural stereotype of Woman as the daughter of Eve, source of all humankind's woes, lives on for many women in their families, their culture, and often their religious institutions. Many battered women report turning to a pastor for help, only to be asked, "What did you do to make him beat you up?" After such a response, few turn to the church again.[22]

Our culture too exploits violence. Our favorite forms of entertainment are often fantasies of violence, many of which depend upon the depiction or threat of violence against women, usually by one or more men. Fairy tales and television shows demonstrate the close association between eroticism and the victimization of women; the damsel in distress is sexually exciting.[23] A multi-million dollar pornography industry dramatizes indignities, brutalization, and torture inflicted upon women, once again by men. Similarly, we sell millions of dollars worth of products through advertisements using female bodies, often in attitudes of adoration, passivity, or actual subjugation toward attractive men. This distortion of human love violates both male and female personhood.

Violence toward women includes rape, both at home and in society. One hundred seventy-five thousand rapes of women, girls, and female infants (as young as six months) are reported yearly. For every rape recorded, the FBI estimates another ten are not.[24] Women find their words, actions, manner of dress, freedom of movement, and choice of living quarters influenced by their constant awareness that they are always vulnerable to sexual attack. Few who have not experienced this habit of mind can comprehend it fully, and the distortions of personhood or behavior produced in women and girls—often at a very early age—cannot be underestimated. In addition, over 70 percent of all women report being victimized by sexual harassment in the workplace[25]—an experience which is again often related to their customary powerlessness in relation to men in positions of authority.

[21] Yahraes. See also Beverly Jacobson, "The Fight to End Wife Beating," *Civil Rights Digest*, Summer, 1977.
[22] David Trembley, "Breaking the Silence," *Christianity and Crisis*, February 21, 1983. See also "Abused Women: Clergy and Church Cannot Cope," *National Catholic Reporter*, June 6, 1980.
[23] Marcia Liebman, "Some Day My Prince Will Come: Female Acculturation Through the Fairytale," *College English*, Vol. 34, 1972, pp. 383–95.
[24] "Myths and Facts . . . ," UPCUSA. See also "Beware of Child Molesters," *Newsweek*, August 9, 1982; and Judith L. Pavlich, "A Crack in the Mirror," *A.D. Magazine*, undated. (This last is distributed by the United Church of Christ Commission for Racial Justice as part of its materials on child abuse.)
[25] Figures based on a study by Lyn Farley, quoted in "Sexual Violence," *JSAC Grapevine*, Vol 11, # 3, September, 1979.

Economically, politically, and culturally, women have not experienced the equality to which God has created them. Much of our culture itself does violence to girls and women, damaging their bodies and their self-esteem with effects which may be lifelong. Just as one instance of domestic violence can establish the balance of family power for a lifetime, so constant reminders of women's powerlessness in society reinforce the dependency which subjects them to violence. Even expressions of Christianity have perpetuated these sexual inequalities in the family forms they have established and upheld, insisting on a hierarchy of male over female and adults over children.

The close association between women and violence is our heritage. But violence begets violence, in an almost unending chain. It is for us, as a church, to rectify this injustice by acting to end this evil.

IV. BIBLICAL AND THEOLOGICAL RATIONALE

The profound significance of the sacredness of God's creation in human beings underlies any theological response to physical and sexual violence. God's creation includes women, created equally in God's own image and equally deserving of the abundant life promised in the Gospels. To affirm, as some have done, that the Bible intends women for subordination and suffering, is to distort and misunderstand the thrust of our heritage. Believing in the goodness and equality of men and women in the created order, we must testify that any unnecessary suffering—particularly the physical or sexual abuse of any person—is a blasphemy before God and a grave injustice in our midst.

The psalmists spoke strong words to condemn violence between intimates:

> My heart is in anguish within me,
> the terrors of death have fallen upon me.
> Fear and trembling come upon me.
> and horror overwhelms me. . . .
> It is not an adversary who deals insolently with me—
> then I could hide from him.
> But it is you, my equal,
> my companion, my familiar friend.
> We used to hold sweet converse together;
> within God's house we walked in fellowship.
> —Psalm 55:4–5, 12–14

Similarly, the prophets repeatedly condemned the exploitation or use of violence against women and children when they lamented that "women are ravished in Zion [Lam. 5:11]," or that evil persons "have ripped up women with child in Gilead, that they might enlarge their border [Amos 1:13]," or that "the women of my people you drive out from their pleasant houses;

from their young children you take away my glory for ever [Mic. 2:9]." Such suffering is clearly as an evil in their eyes.

The Old Testament custom of providing for the widow, orphan and stranger was intended to protect the most vulnerable in Hebrew society, who had lost the protection of a family unit. In our day, the most vulnerable persons in our society are still most frequently and most damagingly the victims of violence: The institutional and attitudinal response to and the delivery of services to certain groups in our society is inferior to the response given to others and extends the agony of the victims.

Unfortunately, the scripture and tradition of the Christian faith are a double-edged sword for women and children. On the one hand, acts of violence against them are condemned as sinful. But on the other, women and children were regarded as property—at the mercy of husband or father. Hence, stories of the rape, mutilation, and murder of women or children are common in scripture, and often leave the impression that these are normal acts. The most frequently expressed Old Testament attitude related to violence against women is concern for the degree of damage in terms of their property value. Thus our religious tradition, with its patriarchal bias, often seems an ambiguous resource for addressing the relationship of violence and women.

We are people of the New Covenant; Jesus' teachings call us to oppose violence and abuse at all levels of our life. His attitude toward women and children was one of compassion and caring, and his outrage at the abuse he saw in the Temple surely parallels our outrage at violence against the most sacred of temples, the human person.

We are called by our Baptism to respond to that abuse, for by Baptism, we are One in the body of Christ. When any member of that body is abused or violated, the whole of Christ's body is injured. As members of that body, we are called to seek justice, but not revenge, to righteous anger, but not blind rage. We are called to works of compassion, justice, and mercy; we are called to pastoral and prophetic ministries in response to victims of violence. We are called as a Church to be a sanctuary for those who are abused.

Jesus foreshadowed this ministry in his story of the Good Samaritan, who cared for one victimized by the violence of his society. Among us today the victims of violence and abuse lie by the side of the road: beaten, humiliated, bruised, and exploited. Too often the Church, like the Priest and the Levite of the Gospel story, has passed by on the other side. We are called to be the Samaritan—to support, shelter, love, and heal those who are victims of violence of this world.

V. STATEMENT OF CHRISTIAN CONVICTION

We are people of the New Covenant. We are all members of the human family of God and each of us should be loved and affirmed as children of God with the same inalienable rights to justice and equality in life. In a violent world, we have declared peace and family life to be priorities for our church. But there can be no peace in the world or in families while violence against women continues.

Therefore, the Fourteenth General Synod calls upon its clergy, laity, and seminarians to educate themselves and others on issues of violence against women, to be advocates for equality between women and men, and to work for the elimination of violence against women.

Proposal for Action Related to the Pronouncement on Violence Against Women

WHEREAS, the Fourteenth General Synod of the United Church of Christ has adopted the Pronouncement on Violence Against Women and since Peace and Family Life are priorities of the United Church of Christ; we experience increasing awareness of violence against women, children and the elderly, and we are called as Christians to be Good Samaritans, to take action on behalf of those who suffer.

THEREFORE, the Fourteenth General Synod of the United Church of Christ calls upon all United Church of Christ churches, Conferences, national Instrumentalities, and other bodies:
—to address the issue of violence against women, by raising consciousness among clergy and laity;
—to work with ecumenical and secular agencies to develop and support hot lines, rape crisis centers, shelters for abused women and children, and programs for abusers;
—to work with schools, churches and hospitals to establish programs to educate prospective parents, parents, and other caretakers of children in the realities of child development, parenting skills, and human sexuality;
—to advocate legislation to protect abused persons and to bring abusers into rehabilitation programs, seeking all prompt, compassionate and just legal remedies for this abuse.

The Fourteenth General Synod calls upon:
—the local United Church of Christ churches to minister to the victims of violence and to their abusers and to develop and support, in cooperation with other agencies, shelters for victims and programs for abusers;
—the Conferences to advocate on the state level for legislation that addresses the issues of violence against women and to advocate for shelters for victims and programs for abusers;
—the Board for Homeland Ministries to recommend and/or publish materials that can be used in churches to help people of all ages understand and oppose sexual and domestic violence, and to examine critically those factors which perpetuate sexual stereotypes destructive

to both female and male personhood and which lead to violence both in families and society; and to encourage schools to examine these issues;

—the Coordinating Center for Women to inform the churches of programs and resources that will increase their understanding of violence against women and coordinate work among Instrumentalities and other bodies in relation to this issue;

—the Office for Church and Society, in collaboration with Instrumentalities, Conferences, and churches, to advocate for legislation that addresses the issues of violence against women;

—the Commission for Racial Justice to address the relationship of cultural, psychosocial, economic, and racial conditions to violence against women and children of color;

—the Office of Communication to publish articles and reports that will inform the churches and community about the issues of violence against women, and to address directly images of violence against women in the media;

—the Board for World Ministries to search out reports concerning the relationship between violence against women and the global exploitation and subordination of women and children and to make the churches aware of that information;

—the Office for Church Life and Leadership to provide pastors with opportunities and resources to enable them to understand issues of violence against women and to initiate a dialogue with our closely related seminaries that would stimulate theological work and encourage preparation of students concerning the issue;

—the Stewardship Council to include in its interpretation of the mission of the whole Church, the Church's work in relation to Violence Against Women.